SUPER S

Crystals are one of Earth's most dazzling treasures. (Obvi!) But they're also believed to emanate mystical frequencies that soothe our emotions and heighten our spiritual awareness. Luckily, there's no need to go cave spelunking or fill your whole home with these magical minerals to start connecting with the power of crystals. The Super Sparkly Crystal Oracle Deck is your handy hookup to the esoteric energies of 50 fab stones—and to add some enchantment to your day!

WHY ARE CRYSTALS SUCH A UNIVERSALLY TREASURED, MAGICAL THING?

It's somewhat obvious why crystals and gems have always been considered prized possessions among royals and everyday people alike. Just look at 'em! What else in nature shimmers, shines, and dazzles quite the way the elements in the crystal kingdom do? They've been coveted not only for their rarity and beauty, but also for their purported metaphysical and healing properties. Crystal healing has been practiced by cultures around the world for thousands of years. Even Cleopatra is said to have used crystal magic in her everyday life.

While the metaphysical magic of crystals isn't backed by science (yet), there are plenty of awe-inspiring qualities about crystals that are. Like, the super strength of diamonds makes them useful in industrial drill bits, dental tools, and smartphones. Similarly, the piezoelectric qualities of quartz means it gets used in watches, GPS devices, and lots of other electronic stuff. Quartz can be also used to store data like a computer chip—and because it vibrates at such precise frequencies, it's crazy good for transmitting frequencies. Under the right conditions, certain crystals can even conduct electricity and generate light.

While crystal healing is still considered a pseudo-science, tons of smart people believe the energy of crystals can subtly influence our bodies' own frequencies—affecting us on physical, emotional, and spiritual levels. Many people also use crystals for manifesting by infusing their intentions into these natural energetic databanks or charging them under the moonlight. Pretty cool, right?

HOW TO USE THIS SUPER SPARKLY DECK...

There are no hard and fast rules when it comes to working with the Super Sparkly Crystal cards. Just close your eyes, think of a question, and randomly pick a card. Trust that you'll naturally be guided to the message that's meant for you—it's like the law of attraction in action!

All you really need to do to start is to shuffle the deck with intention—think about your question as you do so! Then pull a card (or lay out a whole spread), and interpret the cards using the information in this booklet or by drawing upon your own knowledge of crystal magic.

Here are a few sparkly tips & tricks:

✦ Pull a Card of the Day. This is great for daily guidance—and for throwing a fun lil' glitter-bomb over your daily vibes.

✦ Ask a Juicy Q. Need some advice? Looking for a sign? Feel free to ask pointed questions or simply throw a general theme out there . . . Either way, the crystals can help bring inner clarity.

✦ Get Deeper Insight in a Tarot Reading. If a certain card in a tarot spread feels a little ambiguous and you're struggling with its meaning, pull a crystal card to shine some extra glittery light on it.

✦ Do a 3-Card Spread. The Super Sparkly Crystal cards can be used in a multi-card spread, like you might in tarot—past/present/future, work/home/love.

✦ Take It to the Crystal Shop. Crystal shopping can be kind of overwhelming. The wisdom in this deck + your own intuition can help you pick your perfect stone!

But really the most important thing is to have fun, open your mind, and allow all the shimmery crystal magic to shine a mirror into your higher-self!

ALEXANDRITE
Let Your One-of-a-Kind Magic Sparkle

Imposter syndrome and self-consciousness is a trap, baby, so don't fall for it. You are capable of anything you put your mind to—and absolutely worthy of everything good that comes your way. The mystical, multicolored magic of alexandrite is here to remind you of all the one-of-a-kind ways you shimmer and shine.

Make a list of at least ten truly fantastic qualities or special skills you've got—don't be bashful!—then go ahead and read it out loud (or perhaps take this opportunity to add some new bullet-points to your résumé or dating profile, while you're at it!!). Being confident in your strengths and comfortable in your skin is one of the biggest power moves you can make. Let the glory that is you shine bright and start celebrating that magical being looking back at you in the mirror.

AMAZONITE
Trust Your Instincts

It's natural to look outward for guidance, but what if you didn't actually need anyone else's input to settle on the best path/solution/decision/burrito spot?? Amazonite is here to ignite your inner decision-making warrior and gift you the courage to trust your own instincts. If you can quiet all that mental chatter and self-doubt, you'll probably find you already know the answer to some of the questions currently plaguing you.

Sometimes it'll come as a whisper, sometimes it'll be a shout, but if you tune in and listen, you're likely to hear *something* (even if it's just the grumbling of your stomach or the ticking of your clock). The key is to face your truth and be confident enough to stand in it. Say what needs to be said or do what needs to be done without waiting for anyone else to give you the green light. You got this.

AMETHYST
It's All Groovy, Baby

Close your actual eyes, open up your third eye, adorn yourself with an imaginary flower crown, and let's get lost in amethyst's groovy purple haze. This gentle spiritual dynamo calms the nerves and connects you with a sense of tranquility, so its presence is a reminder to find your center and tap into some serious inner peace. Give your spirit a chance to soar instead of stress with some quality "you-time." Nap, doodle, journal, make a vision board, listen to some mood music, or maybe go hug your favorite tree. Amethyst's creative, calming, mystical energy wants to help you find your chill.

AQUAMARINE
Surf the Waves of Your Heart

Step into aquamarine's crystalline waves and take a refreshing dip in your heart's inner current. Named for the cool blue of the ocean, aquamarine energy reflects the depth, clarity, and gentle power of the sea, as well as the cleansing properties of water—so it can help you align deeply with your feelings, find the right words to express them, and generally get yourself into a free 'n' easy flow state. Moving with the tide instead of against it will save you energy and get you places faster, so listen to your heart, honor your feelings, and ride the wave. Who knows, you might meet some wish-granting mermaids along the way!

ARAGONITE
Home Is Where Your Heart Is

The magic of Aragonite is in its ability to connect us to our roots, remind us of what really matters, and encourage us to nurture our home and family life. Perhaps that means hosting a sibling movie night, going through those boxes of memorabilia buried in the garage, or finally planting that herb garden for your parents. The point is to get your hearth & home in order. Also be sure to approach relationships with patience and generosity. Unsweep any domestic grudges or hardships that've been swept under the rug, and assess how the outside world is influencing your internal landscape. OK, now go text all the people you love most and tell them how much they mean to you!

BLACK TOURMALINE
Bad Vibes Begone!

When black tourmaline shows up, it's time to do some spiritual housekeeping and protect yourself from other people's messy energies. This is one of the most protective and negativity-fighting crystals around, and it acts as a mystic force field to keep any unwanted spiritual baggage from penetrating your personal bubble—so trust your gut if someone gives you a bad vibe. If you pick up on any shady side-eyes or less-than-stellar frequencies today, visualize them being sucked into a big black hole, never to be seen again.

BLOODSTONE
Break a Sweat to Get It Done

OK, hot stuff—time to bust some moves and break a sweat in the name of conquering your goals. Bloodstone wants you to get your heart pumping, your energy flowing, and your life force tripping the light fantastic. It's all about vitality, stamina, and forward movement, so take this as your sign to put in some serious work toward whatever you'd like to focus on most. Sitting still and waiting around won't serve you in this moment. So even if it feels like pushing the river to get things streaming in your direction, know that seemingly herculean feats are possible now if you're willing to do the work.

BLUE APATITE
Look Beyond Yourself & Think Big-Pic

It's easy to get caught up in our own daily dramas and personal problems, but the collectivist energy of blue apatite is asking you to look at the bigger picture. How do your current goals and actions benefit the greater good? Do they align with your overall values? Channeling some of your energy into serving others can sometimes make your own (very real) struggles feel smaller and more manageable—at least by a little bit.

This is also a sign to step outside yourself and consider other people's POV in whatever situation you're currently grappling with. Think through the ripple effect your decisions have. Is there someone else who should have more of a say in things? Make sure you give them a chance to weigh in, even if it's just to help pick where to order from for dinner.

CALCITE
Self-Care Yourself

Like a comforting glass of warm milk (or spiked hot cocoa—no judgment!) before bed, curative calcite is here to heal you wherever it hurts!

Always milky in color and soothing in energy, there are many variations of calcite—all equally powerful, but each working on a different vibration.

This card asks you to identify your own sore spots and figure out what areas could use a hot stone-and-CBD-oil massage (literally or metaphorically). Assess yourself for physical, spiritual, or emotional ailments, and focus on healing your own lil' bumps and bruises before worrying about anyone else. And if you really just want to take a mental health day, consider this your self-care permission slip.

CARNELIAN
Channel Your Inner Baddie

Shrinking violet who? Not you! You're the life of the party and the star of the show now, baby, so allow carnelian's confidence-boosting magic to remind you of just how powerful, courageous, and influential you can be.

This fiery-colored crystal lights up your red-hot creative spark and brings out your extroverted tendencies—meaning that it's time to fearlessly assert your visions, opinions, and feelings to the world, like the trailblazin' baddie that you are. Don't hold back when it comes to chasing ambitions or speaking your mind today. The bolder and bigger and badder, the better.

CELESTITE
Let Your Dreams Talk to You

Don't sleep on the power of sleeping! Our nightly snooze-time is an awesome gift for our bodies and minds. We need this daily restorative process to rejuvenate, recharge, and to function properly. There's also spiritual wisdom to be gained during our slumberous travels, and celestite helps connect you to the mystical realm of your dreams.

Our slumber-visions are often super rich with symbolism and meaning, and when this card shows up, it means this may be especially true for you now—so pay attention to what your dreams have to say. If you really listen, your celestial reveries just might blow open some doors and hint at the answers you seek.

CHALCEDONY
Grab the Mic & Speak Your Mind

There's a conversation you need to have with someone, and chalcedony signals that this is a good time to initiate it! Sometimes known as a "speakers stone," chalcedony can inspire you to honestly share what's on your mind without waiting to be asked. Gather your thoughts and feelings, choose your words with eloquence, and craft your tone with diplomacy. A little thoughtful prep will help you get your point across with clarity, and ensure that it's received with open ears and an open heart. Now go get that convo-ball rolling and say what you've gotta say!

CHRYSOCOLLA
Honor Your Experiences

We've all got lots to learn, but we've also got lots to share—so what might you need to teach others? Chrysocolla's sage and mellow energy helps us recognize our unique skill sets and find value in our own experience. Even if you don't think you've done or been through anything super extraordinary, your experiences in this life are yours alone, and no one has the very same POV you do. Believe in your wisdom and consider ways other people might benefit from what you've got to share. You're a lot cooler, worldlier, and more inspirational than you think.

CHRYSOPRASE
If It's Not Your Vibe, Don't Imbibe

Chrysoprase's magical power is in its flexible and ever-mutable vibrations. This crystal is a master of adaptation and going with the flow. But remember, there's a difference between being flexible and attempting a full-blown gymnastics routine. Check in on—and weigh out—just how much adjusting is worth doing to align with your surroundings. If you've been bending over backwards trying to make something fit, it may be time to change direction or seek something else entirely—something that doesn't require so much shifting and squirming and squeezing to make work. Think things through before saying yes to new obligations and distance yourself from stuff that doesn't involve you. Put up a protective force field between yourself and the energies around you. If the energies don't align with your vibe-y, say buh-bye-y!

CITRINE
Tackle That To-Do List

Like morning sun shining through your window as you do a quick stretch and your coffeemaker dings, citrine is your spiritual vitamin C—inspiring positivity, energy, and focus in equal doses. Think of it as the crystal version of a big yellow smiley face. This is your signal that the moment is right—and that you're *totally* ready—to tackle your to-do list and start taking action on your brilliant ideas. Your productivity levels are popping off and a cheery beam of optimism is beginning to shine over the situation at hand. Even if it's just via baby steps, making tangible progress toward your goals can really boost your confidence, so put some pep in your step and get moving! With the zingy energy of citrine on your side, you can accomplish just about anything.

CLEAR QUARTZ
Get Crystal Clear About Your Intentions

The purity and glow of clear quartz can amplify whatever frequencies it comes in contact with—so this is your spirit-call to get in touch with your intentions. The law of attraction wants to work in your favor, but you've gotta get crystal-clear on what you want. Otherwise, you're just that person who got to the front of the line at the cosmic café and still didn't know what drink to order! Dig deep and get to the root of *why* you want what you want. Will that specific job really make all your dreams come true . . . or do you just want financial security? Are you desperate for that specific person to ask you out . . . or are you just craving some cuddle time? When you understand your motivations on a deeper and more honest level, your manifestations will pack a *way* more powerful punch. Now get back in line at the cosmic café and be ready to place that order!

DIAMOND
Crank Up the Positivity

Greetings, your excellency. It's time for the royal treatment! Diamonds are the most highly prized of all precious stones (duh!), and these dazzling jewels are thought to have the power to magnify all the energies around them. That's why it's especially important to focus on the positive when this card shows up! Turn down the negative self-talk and embrace the power of a hopeful outlook. Start by thinking of one thing you're very grateful for—then repeat through the day! Surround yourself with optimistic people and motivating energies. Try to reframe difficult situations as welcome growth experiences. These little efforts can have a big impact on your mindset and manifestation abilities—so watch for signs of your wishes beginning to unfold into a sparkly new reality.

EMERALD
Tend Your Emotional Garden

Emerald's lush green energy nourishes whatever needs nourishing, without giving too much or too little. Perhaps right now your life could benefit from this precious gem's gentle temperance, too? Take some deep breaths and assess the balance of your emotions. Are certain feelings taking up too much space and focus? Are other parts of your heart/soul wilting from lack of attention? Like a plant needs a just-right mix of light, water, soil, and sweet-talking, your emotional life and inner-world require a special regimen to thrive, too. With kindness and care, all things can grow—including your relationships, your self-discipline, or the temperamental fiddle-leaf fig in your living room. Find your emotional equilibrium so you can act from a place of truth, instead of reacting to a feeling that may float on by as quickly as it drifted on in.

FLUORITE
Clear Your Mind & the Rest Will Follow

When fluorite shows up, it's probably time for a mini mental reboot! Start by taking a deep breath, filling those beautiful lungs with a cleansing gust and charging up those beautiful brain cells with a healthy puff of oxygen. Now breathe out, using your intention to release all chaos, confusion, and clutter from your mind. Feels good, right? Fluorite is like that friend who inspires you to clean out your closets and organize your junk drawer. It helps to enhance your intellect and clarify your visions—making you sharper, better, faster, and smarter. Take this card as a sign to fully think things through, lead with logic, and look for creative solutions to any issues.

GARNET
It's All About the Baby Steps

No matter how big or small the task at hand may be, the very first step is always one of the hardest to take. Garnet believes you're ready to quit your procrastinating and rock steady! It's here to give you a gentle trust-push forward, encouraging you to rip off that fear-bandage and tackle something you've been putting off. No more waiting for some magical green light or for the "perfect" moment. No more looking to follow someone else's lead. Just take that first initiative toddle to set things in motion and see what mystical paths lie ahead.

GREEN AVENTURINE
Thank Your Lucky Stars

Fate is on your side now, so make a wish on a shooting star—or a dandelion, heads-up penny, wishing well, ice cream cone, whatever! Just take a chance. The auspicious magic of green aventurine is like getting the best fortune cookie in the world, blessing you with a windfall of good karma and a protective bubble of good luck.

Opportunities may seem to materialize out of thin air, giving you an advantage to secure something special—so grab your favorite lucky charm and head toward your nearest rainbow. If you believe that the universe is coming together to work things out in your favor (it is!), then anything is possible (ditto!).

HEMATITE
Reality Check Yourself

The universe thinks you may need a reality check, so peel those rose-colored filters off your eyeballs and don't look away from what's right in front of you. Dark and shiny hematite helps reflect our true circumstances back to us so we can see things from a more grounded perspective—because while our hopes and dreams can fuel us, having your head in the clouds could cause you to overlook some obvious steps. When you're centered, solidly rooted, and acting from a place of acceptance rather than denial, it's a lot easier to move forward in a way that makes sense. Yay!

IOLITE
Calibrate Your Inner Compass

Sometimes known as the "viking's compass," iolite energy can help people find their way. And perhaps you could use a bit more direction right about now, too (I mean, seriously, who couldn't?). In what areas do you feel lost, uncertain, or out of touch with your purpose? Is your soul's compass struggling to settle on its true north? Wandering aimlessly can be fun, and we don't always have to have a clear objective or ultra-aspirational goal to steer toward. But if you don't figure out where you want to go at some point, you'll always be heading toward an unknown destination, which could take you further away from your heart's true path. Iolite wants you to stop, reorient yourself, and get clear on where you're going and what you want—even if it's just to the nearest mall for some retail therapy and corporate coffee. We're not judging.

JADE
Be the Calm Within the Storm

When things in your life feel like they're spinning out of control, the magic of jade can help you find the calm in the eye of the storm. Now's the time to connect with that peaceful portal in your own life. Because no matter how wild the chaos might seem to get, there is always a place inside you where you can retreat. Jade's energy can help you balance your emotions with your intellect and find a moment of clarity amidst these spiritual tornadoes. Catch your breath, clear your mind, and try to stay calm—because even the craziest storms do eventually pass.

JASPER
Check Yourself
Before You Wreck Yourself

You could probably use a little spiritual refueling right about now, couldn't you? Just in time, jasper's grounding energy is here to envelop you in a calming cocoon of comfort and offer you a cosmic rest stop. Being super on-the-go can be a thrill, but when there are parts of you that need to heal, it's good to slow down and give yourself some extra tenderness and conscious self-care. 'Cause remember, if you keep putting the pedal to the metal on an empty tank, you'll eventually run out of gas—which is a situation no one wants to find themselves in. Now's the time to start taking care of your needs and prioritizing your well-being. Focus on nurturing yourself with things that feel healthy, practical, and pleasurable.

KYANITE
Tune In to Your Inner-Truth

When the lights go out and everything goes black, it may feel like you have no way to see what's in front of you. But if you stay calm and allow your eyes to adjust, you'll realize that you can make out quite a bit more than you'd think. The magic of kyanite is like putting on a pair of night-vision goggles and turning up your psychic powers, helping you to connect with the invisible influences that lie beyond the surface of your current situation. Consider yourself a spiritual spelunker now, seeing and feeling and vibing your way through a cave full of secrets and spiders and all sorts of mystical wonders. The signs of truth are right in front of you, perhaps hidden in plain view—and you are fully capable of discovering the answers you seek.

LABRADORITE
Believe In Your Magic

Few gems are believed to possess more mystical powers than the almighty labradorite, a crystal with all the shimmering hues and awesome mystique of the aurora borealis itself. This regal crystal is here to awaken the wisdom of your deepest self and bring those spiritual depths to the surface. Instead of letting your intellect or emotions make today's decisions, tap into your soul's inner-knowing and see what your intuition has to say. Inexplicable magic is swirling around you, dancing through the sky like the Northern Lights and connecting you with your divine power.

LAPIS LAZULI
Get Real & Own Your Truth

It's totally natural to tell ourselves stories and fill in the gaps of our experiences with some colorful assumptions—who doesn't love a juicy narrative arc? But getting lost in our emotional (and sometimes wounded) projections can disconnect us from reality. Lapis lazuli, with its rich blue hue, draws us toward truth, connects us with our memories, and sharpens our minds. Being honest with others starts with being honest with ourselves, which is hard sometimes. This crystal wants you to clear out the fantasy fluff, face the facts, and listen to your deepest truth with open-to-honesty ears.

LARIMAR
Cool It Down, Babe

Feeling fired up and blazing with passion is great—but right now, the cooling vibes of larimar want you to channel your inner Mona Lisa.

Larimar energy is cool, calm, and collected, so when this card shows up, you can trust that acting from a place of serenity and stillness will yield the best results. So before you have that super-important talk with your boss or S.O., practice chilling out, calming down, and putting up some healthy emotional boundaries. While you certainly don't want the heat of your enthusiasm to burn out, you also don't want it to end up scalding you.

LEPIDOLITE
Find Your Quietude

Stress and intrusive thoughts might be keeping you up at night. So annoying, right? (Why can't our sweetest, fluffiest fantasies ever keep us up at night instead? Sigh.) Fortunately, the tranquil energy of lepidolite is here to calm your racing heart and wash away your anxiety. Drawing this soothing card is like applying a mineral mud mask to your soul. So close your eyes and take a big belly breath. Then, when you're ready, look at the stressors in your life—but instead of stressing about them, find some intentional ways to bring grounding moments of calm into your day. A bubble bath or early night in might be just the thing you need to restore some tranquility.

MALACHITE
Break Up With Toxic Old Patterns

The protective yet change-inducing magic of malachite is here to help you safely outgrow your energetic barriers using the three C's: consciousness, clarity, and confidence. The thing about patterns is that they often develop without us ever fully realizing it. Sneaky, huh? And once these repetitive motions create grooves in your life—smooth and cozy paths resulting from habitual choices—following the same ol' sequences starts to feel like the easiest option. (Kind of like the urge to put on sweats, order a pizza, and scroll on your phone for six hours after getting home from work.)

But not all of these comfy, unconscious rhythms beat to the vibration of your highest self, and you should be aligning with frequencies that support your evolution, not hinder it! This card is your catalyst to officially break out of these patterns and give your heart the freedom to build healthy new dynamics in their place.

MOLDAVITE
Buckle Up, Buttercup!

If it feels like you've suddenly been hit by lightning or abducted by aliens, try to trust that these freak occurrences might actually be a good thing—because the ultra-transformative magic of moldavite has fully got your back. This rock star of a gem formed when a meteorite crashed into earth millions of years ago, bestowing it with an out-of-this-world energy that helps us vibrate beyond what we think is possible within our planet's sphere. Its extraterrestrial power triggers transformation at a warp-speed pace. Breaking out of the familiar and leveling up in light-years is the deal here. The universe—your universe—is chock-full of pixie dust and limitless possibilities, so open your heart to the idea that you can live a life beyond your wildest imagination. Buckle up and say yes to the adventure!

MOONSTONE
Roll With the Tides of Your Heart

Just as the moon waxes and wanes and changes form throughout the month, so do our feelings—which is why it's so important to give those babies some room to dance, swim, and shapeshift! Moonstone wants to coax your vulnerable side out from its cozy, protective cave, and allow your emotions to come out and party in the moonlight. That means all of them: the painful ones, the tricky ones, and the ones you'd rather eat glass than admit to publicly. Take note of the phase of the moon and make an offering to trust life's cycles. By letting your heart roll with the ebb and flow of life's turning tides today, you'll find that it's easier to let things go and embrace the mysterious magic of your shadow self.

MOSS AGATE
Trust the (Growth) Process

There's a real thrill that comes along with planting a new seed or a magic bean, but you can't expect it to sprout into a full-fledged beanstalk overnight! Moss agate's earthy, fertile, green energy reminds you that growth is definitely in process . . . even if it's still a little bud that hasn't found a crack in the sidewalk to push up through just yet. Pace yourself and try to calm down your desire for quick results by focusing on the bigger-picture, longer-term progress that's taking place under the surface. Your seedlings need time before they can start bearing flowers or fruit—but you can trust they'll be blooming down the line.

OBSIDIAN
Grieve What's Gone

Loss is a natural part of being alive and being in love—because when we open our hearts to all the wonderful people, animals, and things that life has to offer, we also have to accept that we'll eventually have to say goodbye to them, too.

But just because grief is natural doesn't mean it's fun or easy. It isn't. It *hurts*. And it's hard. And there's no magic wand that anyone can wave to make it disappear. As much as you might wish for a quick fix, there's no secret shortcut through the process. The only way out is through. Allow obsidian—in all its depth and darkness—to help you accept your losses, appreciate your past, and move forward into a new part of your journey with all the knowledge you've gained along the way. It may not happen overnight, but if you let yourself truly mourn whatever has ended, your grief will someday feel less like pain and more like a lasting reminder of love.

ONYX
Find Light in the Darkness

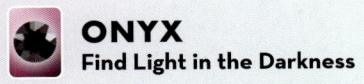

Spoiler alert: life isn't all sparkles & tacos & fluffy lil' kittens. And not to be a total downer or anything, but you're setting yourself up for disappointment if you expect it to be. While it's generally good to look at the bright side, the deep, dark energy of onyx reminds us to honor the balance between positive and negative that is the reality of human existence. There's always some good in the bad—and some bad in the good. Instead of running from the darkness in your life, find ways to accept and embrace it as a temporary visitor. The shadows have lessons, and they can help us appreciate the light.

OPAL
Look for the Rainbow in Everything

The milky depth of the opal stone reflects the full prism of the rainbow—offering satisfying proof that the entire spectrum of color exists within everything, if you just look at it from the right angle. Are you able to see this incredible range of hues in your current situation and reflection? Or is your spiritual TV set stuck in standard-definition black-and-white without you even realizing it? Everything has a little something to teach you today, and every interaction you have or person you bump into can help to reveal something important about yourself. As above, so below—know what I mean? Take note of how your surroundings are shaping your inner landscape, and be aware of the ways in which your inner rainbow can radiate out and affect the world around you, too.

PERIDOT
Set Those Heavy Bricks Down Already

What energetic burdens are you carrying around right now? What onerous feelings are you holding onto? The rich green magic of peridot is here to help to lighten your load. Bad things do happen sometimes, and our circumstances will inevitably affect our overall well-being—but it is decidedly *not* your responsibility to drag sadness, jealousy, anger, or fear around with you forever. You are not an emotional baggage cart, and your spiritual muscles need a break! Take an inventory of what's weighing you down, then when you're ready, resolve to gently unload some (or all!) of those heavy items. Release them with love and allow yourself to regain a sense of lightness in your heart. You deserve that.

PYRITE
Bring On the Abundance

You don't need a trillion bucks to *feel* like a trillion bucks. Really. Abundance isn't about wealth or fancy things—though that's admittedly hard to remember when we're lost in a sea of celebrity-worshipping and overly-curated social media posts. Real abundance means having a mindset that recognizes beauty in the little things and savoring the profound richness of everyday experience, as well as the glorious vastness of the universe. You can start flexing your abundance-muscles right now by immersing yourself in simple pleasures and feeling gratitude for all that you have. Bonus: when your brain's abundance-mode is activated, you're likely to attract *more* of that same magic!

RHODOCHROSITE
Heal That Broken Heart

Being sad sucks and heartbreak hurts. Like, a lot. And when you're down in the dumps, it can feel like every sappy song on the radio is taunting you and every happy face you see is smiling to spite you. The magic of rhodochrosite is like a gentle salve, here to soothe your soul and remind you that despite any heaviness weighing you down, there's still plenty of love and happiness in the world—and it's going to shine its light on you again (and again). With the healing energy of this crystal in your orbit, it's an auspicious time to give yourself some TLC and remind yourself that it's safe to open your heart again. Journal out your feelings, talk to a loved one about your heartaches, or bake a warm apple pie to have all to yourself. Don't forget the vanilla ice cream.

ROSE QUARTZ
Let Your Rose-Colored Heart Lead the Way

Stop and smell the rose quartz, babe. It probably smells like hearts and butterflies and chocolate candies because this card indicates that romance and heart-flutters are near! Rose quartz helps you find the dreamy beauty in just about anything—like enjoying the pink glow of the sunset out your window during an otherwise miserable and traffic-filled evening commute. Its gentle energy also brings out the most beautiful tenderness in relationships, and it can coax compassion out of the deepest corners of your heart, allowing you to feel unconditional love for yourself and others alike. Put your guard down and trust in this rose-colored crystal magic today. Now is a time to open your heart and let love lead the way.

RUBY
You're the Queen Bee, Honey

Lucky you! Today you're blessed by a visit from one of the rarest and most elegant of all precious gems. The scarlet rays of the ruby are shining their sultry red glow all over you . . . and sprinkling a little bit of sugar, spice, and *bow-chicka-wow-wow* energy into your life. This luxurious crystal is purportedly an aphrodisiac, upping your seductiveness levels and making you irresistible to every object of your desire. Ruby invites you to indulge your sensual side, while reminding you that you don't chase—you attract. You draw things you want right into your arms, like bees to clover or moths to a flame. But how, you ask? The first step is to believe that you deserve the best in all the land. Because baby, you do.

SAPPHIRE
Seek Wisdom, Dear Grasshopper

Sapphire is one of the four esteemed precious stones (aka it's *very* fancy). Even cooler? Like a wise old sage in crystal form, it's got its own special brand of wisdom to impart—and it's asking you to welcome new ways of thinking. This could be through meditation, talks with friends, a trip to the library, or whatever else your thing might be!

Learning new stuff and tapping into our innate knowing is necessary for basic survival as well as our divine/psychic/spiritual evolution. Sapphire helps to activate our higher consciousness, making room for growth and paving the way for freedom. Right now, you're a conduit for all sorts of mind-expanding info, so keep those channels tuned!

SELENITE
Cleanse Your Energy Field

What's hiding in the shadows of your heart? Are you being totally honest with yourself? Has some energetic gunk accumulated in your aura?

Like the rays of a full moon or a giant disco ball, selenite helps illuminate anything that's been tucked away in the darkness or swept out of sight. Also known as the "goddess stone," selenite's soothing glow gently bathes things in lightness and purifies them from the inside out. It helps remind us to clean our spiritual closets and clear out all the clunky and cumbersome crap that may be keeping us from feeling free. Take a long shower, tidy up your room, light a candle, and call forth some fresh, squeaky-clean energy.

SHUNGITE
Detoxify Your Life

Are you stuck in a toxic cycle? Or feeling consumed by some less-than-stellar habits? Shungite wants to help you sweat it out of your system, literally and metaphysically. This ancient crystal is a cleansing queen. It's believed to help our bodies offset harmful energies from electronics and tech devices, as well as support all sorts of other detoxifying efforts, too.

So whether you need to take a break from doom scrolling, splurge-y shoe shopping, or too many after-work happy hour drinks, make a commitment to eighty-six a vice from your life and give yourself the space to let something more productive flourish in its place. (And if you're in the mood to take a sauna, drink some wheatgrass, get a deep-tissue massage, or talk to a therapist, so much the better!)

SMOKY QUARTZ
Put Your Own Oxygen Mask on First

Where there's smoke, there's usually some sort of fire—whether it's a four-alarm deal or just someone lighting a candle for their full moon ritual. Either way, the grounded energy of smoky quartz is here to shield you from the flames.

But this protective gem also wants you to know that *you* possess the superpower of self-preservation, and now's a good time to use it. Take extra care to guard against careless mistakes, heed red flags, and avoid sketchy people/places/things. Be aware of your blind spots and vulnerabilities and watch your back. Keep your antennae perked to detect any signs of danger—at least for the moment, until the clouds have blown south and things look a little less hazy.

SUGILITE
Keep It Simple & Sweet

Sweet as sugar, the magic of sugilite bodes well for all endeavors, bringing forth a likelihood of positive alignments and magical synchronicities. But if you're overly caught up in minor details—like the fact the ice cream shoppe may have forgotten to add rainbow sprinkles to your otherwise chef's-kiss-worthy sundae—then you won't be able to enjoy the deliciousness of what's right in front of you.

Strip your situations down of all the fluffy complications and start simplifying things. By cutting out the clutter and paring things down to their most basic forms, you'll feel lighter, freer, and ready to take flight onto cotton candy clouds. And sugilite's sweetness will be by your side.

SUNSTONE
Embrace Your Main Character Energy

You're like a spiritual solar panel today, capable of absorbing every glimmering ray of light you come in contact with and converting it into your own personal power source. Sunstone awakens your soul's inner power (your *soul-ar* power, if you will!), filling you with drive, inspiration, and the courage to share your inner light with the world.

You're *always* going to be the hero of your story, so it's time to start believing in yourself and writing your own happy ending. Or feel-good new beginning. Or excitement-filled plot twist. It's up to you, babe. You're the main character, so your future can be as bright as a summer's day is long. And with sunstone on your side, you are truly the center of everyone's orbit.

TIGER'S EYE
You've Earned Your Stripes

Have you felt afraid of going after what you want? Standing up for yourself? Taking a risk? Of course you have—you're a human, after all. But you're also braver and more powerful than you think, and now you've got the eye of the tiger on your side (cue guitars!). This is the moment to harness the majestic courage of tiger's eye and show everyone you've earned your stripes.

When you tame your fears and step into your own strength, it puts people and things under your spell. Like a regal jungle kitty closing in on its prey, focus on exactly what you want and allow all the background noise to fade away. Now make your move, tiger.

TURQUOISE
WWYISD?
(What Would Your Ideal Self Do?)

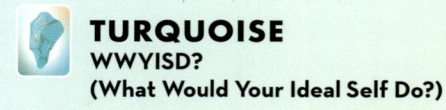

Our thoughts actually have *serious* clout when it comes to causing ripple effects in our reality (just consider the power of a placebo, for example!). So, visualizing your most fantastical fantasies coming to life is so much more than just a silly, pipe-dreamin', hopeless romantic dreamer's way to pass the afternoon. Imagination-enhancing turquoise is a gorgeous reminder that sometimes if you can change the way you think, you can change the way you live, too.

Pretend your life is a virtual-reality role-playing game and your ideal self is the main character—then jump right on into this new mindset. Try to make decisions as if you were already living your dreams. Then watch as the dream-chips fall into place.